JIM CARREY

by
Jill C. Wheeler

Visit us at
www.abdopub.com

Published by ABDO Publishing Company, 4940 Viking Drive, Edina, MN 55435. Copyright ©2001 by Abdo Consulting Group, Inc. International copyrights reserved in all countries. No part of this book may be reproduced in any form without written permission from the publisher.

Printed in the United States.

Graphic Design: John Hamilton
Photo Credits:
   20th Century Fox and Conundrum Entertainment, p. 52
   AP/Wide World, p. 38, 41, 45, 47, 49, 53, 59
   Corbis, p. 5, 6, 7, 12, 13, 21, 27, 51, 55, 57, 60-61, 63
   MPCA and New Line Cinema, p. 44
   New Line Cinema and Dark Horse Entertainment, p. 44
   Shooting Stars, p. 10, 15, 19, 25, 29, 33, 37, 43
   Time Pix, p. 9, 16, 22, 31, 35
   Universal Pictures and Imagine Entertainment, p. 48
   Warner Brothers and Morgan Creek Productions, p. 40

Library of Congress Cataloging-in-Publication Data
Wheeler, Jill C., 1964-
    Jim Carrey / Jill C. Wheeler.
       p. cm. -- (Star Tracks)
    Includes index.
    ISBN 1-57765-556-7
       1. Carrey, Jim, 1962--Juvenile literature. 2. Motion picture
actors and actresses--United States--Biography--Juvenile literature.
3. Comedians--United States--Biography--Juvenile literature. [1.
Carrey, Jim, 1962- 2. Comedians. 3. Actors and actresses.] I. Title.
II. Series.

PN2287.C278 W49 2001
791.43'028'092--dc21
[B]
                                                    00-050263

CONTENTS

AN INSPIRATION

ON MARCH 6, 1995, MILLIONS OF Americans tuned in to watch the American Comedy Awards. The annual show honors entertainers who have done a great job making people laugh.

Each year the show gives a special Creative Achievement Award for one person's lifetime body of work. That year, comic Rodney Dangerfield received the award. Dangerfield spent years perfecting his craft. He still likes to joke that he never gets any respect.

The comedian who presented Dangerfield's award also spent years working with little respect. In fact, it was only the year before that he finally became a household name. He was Jim Carrey.

In presenting the award, Jim told how Dangerfield had helped him get started in entertainment. Rodney asked Jim to open for many of his shows in places like Las Vegas. Jim told the audience how Rodney had inspired him to keep going even when success seemed a million miles away.

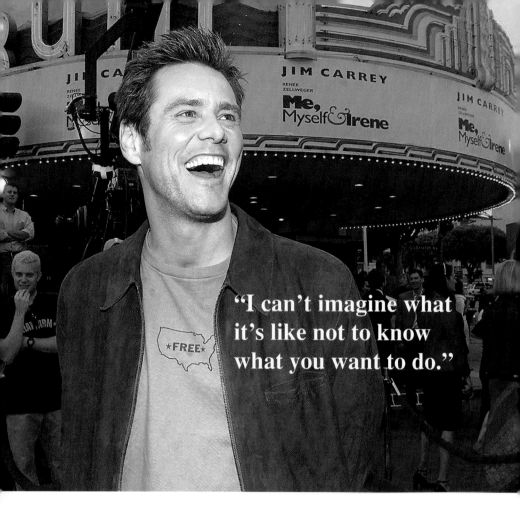

"I can't imagine what it's like not to know what you want to do."

"Sometimes the only thing that kept me going was the thought that Rodney made it when he was in his 50s," said Jim. He added that he knew he was doing well when he heard Rodney laughing offstage.

Today Jim Carrey has moved from an opening act to a starring role. His outrageous performance in 1994's *Ace Ventura: Pet Detective* rocketed him to fame. He earned a record $20 million for *The Cable Guy*. That made him the highest paid comedic actor at that time. His journey to stardom

"I knew what I wanted from the time I was a little kid."

was anything but smooth or swift. Yet it was always exactly what he wanted to do.

"I can't imagine what it's like not to know what you want to do," he said. "People come out of college not knowing. I can't imagine that. It must be a horrible feeling. I knew what I wanted from the time I was a little kid."

JIMMY GENE

THE

STRING

BEAN

JAMES EUGENE CARREY WAS BORN ON
January 17, 1962, in Newmarket, Ontario, Canada.
Newmarket is a suburb of Toronto. He was the
youngest of four children born to Percy and
Kathleen Carrey.

Percy had been a jazz musician before he
started a family. Sometimes Kathleen sang with
his band. When their first daughter, Pat, was born,
Percy sold his saxophone. He took an accounting
job instead. It hurt him to give up jazz. Still, he
felt he could better provide for his family with a
steady job. He had a fine-tuned sense of humor
and always kept people laughing. He also loved to
play practical jokes on his children.

Kathleen Carrey was a former hairdresser. For most of Jim's life, she said she was in pain. She would lie in bed for days taking painkillers and watching television. Jim felt she sometimes pretended to be sick to get attention. As a child, she had not received much attention from her parents, who had problems with alcohol. Jim tried to cheer her up with his humor, though it seldom worked.

Throughout his young life, Jim used humor to ease tensions and make friends. As a toddler, he would make faces during mealtimes instead of eating. His oldest sister recalls that he "always made faces instead of eating. He'd make us laugh, and Mom would get mad because he wouldn't eat." He even became thin from not eating. Later his classmates teased him with the nickname "Jimmy Gene the String Bean."

"Throughout his young life, Jim used humor to ease tensions and make friends."

As Jim got older, he continued playing family clown. Whenever the Carrey family had guests, they could count on Jim to entertain. Still, Jim credits his father as being the best comedian in the family. The Carrey household frequently rocked with laughter, practical jokes, and even food fights.

In second grade, Jim did an imitation that had his entire class laughing. "I remember starting out imitating records in the back of the classroom," he

"Jim quickly realized he had a special gift."

said in an interview. "When the teacher singled me out and tried to make me feel embarrassed by saying, 'Get up and do that in front of the whole class,' it marked the end of a normal life." Jim was more than happy to do his "routine" in front of the whole class. The teacher enjoyed it so much she let him do it in the school Christmas pageant.

Jim quickly realized he had a special gift. He would spend hours in front of the mirror making faces and practicing impersonations. When his parents needed to punish him, they couldn't send him to his room. He enjoyed that too much. Instead they had to force him to go play with other kids.

Jim often was one of the first in his class to finish his schoolwork. Then he would get to work making the other kids laugh. Sometimes that disrupted class. His seventh grade teacher made a special deal with him. She said if he would be quiet for the first part of class, he could have the "stage" for the last 15 minutes. That suited Jim just fine. It also helped him make friends.

"Until I was in junior high school, I didn't know how to make friends," he said. "Then I found out that the things I did at home to entertain people also cracked up everyone at school. I started acting goofy and everyone wanted to hang out with me. Acting goofy became my entire motivation for living."

When not entertaining, Jim liked to lock himself in a closet and write songs and poetry and draw pictures. Some of his pencil sketches won awards at art exhibitions. Later in life he would have one of his songs recorded by the musical group Tuck & Patti.

"Acting goofy became my entire motivation for living."

NIGHT

S H I F T

JIM'S LIFE CHANGED DRASTICALLY

when he was just 14 years old. His father lost his job at the accounting firm where he had worked for more than 25 years. Nearly 50 years old, Percy had a hard time finding another job. He looked and looked unsuccessfully for another accounting job. Finally he took a job as a janitor at the Titan Wheels factory in Scarborough, Ontario. One of the reasons he took the job was so his family could live in the factory housing next door.

In time the entire Carrey family was working in the factory. Jim spent the day in school, then had to clean restrooms at the factory for another eight hours. Most schooldays he could barely keep his eyes open. His schoolwork suffered, and his grades plummeted. He became angry at the world for what had happened.

The rest of the family was unhappy as well. Jim's grandparents became very critical of his father. "My grandparents were alcoholics," he told *Parade* magazine. "My grandfather would get my dad in a corner every Christmas and tell him what a loser he was because he didn't have a job. My father would just sit there and turn purple with anger."

Jim learned to imitate his grandparents as soon as they left the house, which made his father laugh. "My father would be so relieved," Jim recalled. "It was as if I pulled the pressure plug when I went into this routine."

"It was as if I pulled the pressure plug when I went into this routine."

DISASTROUS

DEBUT

EVEN WHEN THE CARREY FAMILY'S LIFE was at its darkest, Percy Carrey had faith in his son's talent. When Jim was only 14, Percy arranged for him to appear at a Toronto comedy club. Together, Jim and Percy wrote up the routine. Kathleen insisted her son wear a yellow polyester suit on stage for his performance. She thought that was what people in the entertainment field wore. Jim couldn't drive yet, so his father drove him to Yuk-Yuk's Komedy Kabaret the night of his first performance.

At his first comedy club performance, Jim was booed off the stage before his five minutes were up.

Jim recalls that things at the club couldn't have gone any worse. His yellow suit was not in style at all. The crowd didn't laugh at his jokes or impersonations. Worst of all, even the club owner heckled him. Jim was literally booed off the stage before his five minutes were up. He had to go back to working in the factory. Eventually, he dropped out of high school because he was just too tired all the time.

Meanwhile, Percy realized the factory was taking a terrible toll on his family. Where once there had been laughter and jokes, now there was bitterness and hatred. He decided to leave Titan Wheels. That meant, however, that the family had to live in a battered yellow Volkswagen van. The Carreys spent nearly a year living in a van as the family members looked for work.

NO
ASSURANCES

FOR JIM, FINDING WORK MEANT GOING
back on stage. He refused to let the disaster at
Yuk-Yuk's defeat him. He had been practicing to
be a comedian all his life. He knew no other way
to find work. He also remembered his father's
shattered dreams of being a musician. He would
take whatever risks necessary to live his dream.
"Life offers no assurance," he said later. "So you
might as well do what you're really passionate
about."

Jim began honing his act and trying it out at
other clubs. Two years after he'd been booed off
the stage, he returned to Yuk-Yuk's. He was only
16, but this time he brought the house down. The
club owner who had heckled him before was
amazed at the change. He realized Jim's talent was
out of the ordinary.

Jim made new friends as he made the rounds of the Toronto comedy clubs. One fellow comedian who became a close friend was Wayne Flemming. Flemming offered to drive Jim home one night. He was astonished when Jim told him to stop at the end of the street. There was only a yellow van there. Jim explained, "This is where we all sleep."

Critics as well as fans began to take notice of Jim Carrey. He started to earn money for his comedy as other members of his family found jobs. Eventually, they were able to move back into a real house. Another big break for Jim came when comedian Rodney Dangerfield signed him to open for Dangerfield's Canadian tour.

For Jim, there was only one logical next step: Hollywood. He had succeeded in Canada. Yet his work in Canada would never make him the kind of star he wanted to be. At age 19, he was ready to try for the big time.

"Life offers no assurance, so you might as well do what you're really passionate about."

Jim Carrey at the premiere of Dr. Seuss's How the Grinch Stole Christmas, *with comedian Rodney Dangerfield November 8, 2000, in Los Angeles.*

HELLO,

HOLLYWOOD

COMPARED TO TORONTO, LOS ANGELES was another world. Jim arrived and found a room in an old hotel in a rundown section of town. He tried calling some of the comedians he'd met in Canada. Most didn't want to help him. Finally he found a struggling songwriter with an extra bedroom to rent.

He wasted no time in performing at Los Angeles area comedy clubs. As in Canada, people noticed him almost immediately. Audiences and other comics marveled at his talents, especially his celebrity impersonations. He was especially excited to perform at The Comedy Store. That club had launched many a comedian's career, including Robin Williams. Many people saw a touch of Robin Williams' manic energy in the lanky Canadian.

Jim started out earning as little as $25 a night. Yet it wasn't long before he was earning a good living doing comedy. Unlike many other struggling stars who finally "make it," Jim didn't let his success change him. He didn't waste his money on lavish homes or limousines. Nor did he appear stuck-up.

He took the opportunity to have his parents come live with him in Los Angeles. Yet the stress of taking care of them took its toll. He finally had to ask them to move back to Canada.

Jim had become the king of impersonations. However, that was not where he wanted to be. He wanted to work on his act even more. He wanted to expand beyond impersonating people. He wanted to develop an act that showcased his other talents. He knew he would be risking failure again. He also knew what not taking risks had done to his father's dreams.

Once again, Jim got to work. He watched old movies and videos of famous comedians. He especially liked Peter Sellers, Jerry Lewis and his idol, Jimmy Stewart. He took notes on what they did and why it worked. He often drove up to Los Angeles' Mulholland Drive where he could look out over the city. He vowed that one day he would become a star.

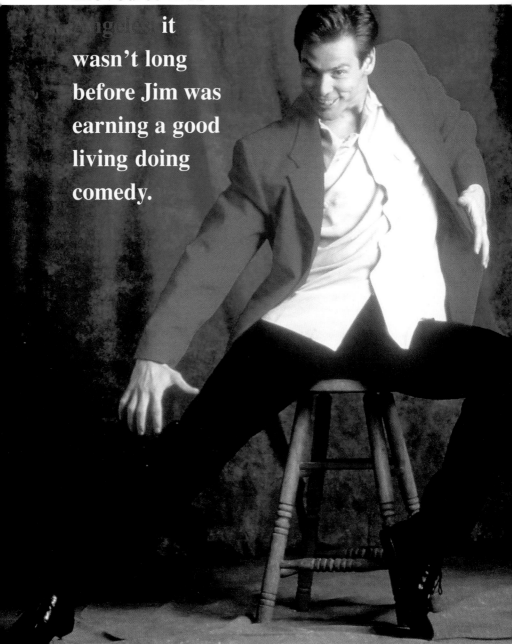

Once he moved to Los Angeles, it wasn't long before Jim was earning a good living doing comedy.

A
NEW ACT

WHILE PERFORMING AT THE COMEDY Store, Jim met a young waitress named Melissa Wormer. The two fell in love, and they were married on March 28, 1986. The following year they became parents of a daughter, Jane. Now Jim had another role as husband and father. It seemed to help calm and ground him. It also gave him confidence.

After two years of practice, Jim was ready to unveil his new act on the L.A. comedy scene. This act showcased Jim's amazing talents at improvisation. Improvisation is when a comedian makes up a routine on the spur of the moment, often from an audience suggestion. He blended quick thinking with fluid body movements and slapstick skills to create a new kind of act. Audiences never knew what they'd see from him. Sometimes it was hilarious. Other times it failed miserably. But it was always intriguing.

One person who was intrigued by Jim was the president of NBC Entertainment. In 1982, he saw Jim perform at The Comedy Store. He decided the Canadian was the perfect person to star in a new series he was developing. It was called *The Duck Factory.*

In the 1984 show, Jim played a cartoonist working in an animation studio. The show was unique in blending live-action performers with animated characters. Unfortunately, Jim played a straight role. His character didn't enable him to use his full range of talents. Jim did well with the material he was given. However the show failed after only 13 episodes. Jim took it in stride. "I always kind of believed in miracles," he said. "Some way, something was going to pop out."

"Jim blended quick thinking with fluid body movements and slapstick skills to create a new kind of act."

"I always kind of believed in miracles."

BIT
PARTS

THE BIG MIRACLE JIM WAS LOOKING FOR was still years away. In the meantime, he landed bit parts in several movies. He first appeared on the silver screen in 1984's forgettable *Finders Keepers*. He followed that with small parts in the 1985 vampire comedy *Once Bitten*. In 1986, he won a part as Nicolas Cage's friend in *Peggy Sue Got Married*. He and Cage became good friends during the course of the production.

Even Clint Eastwood took notice of the young actor. After seeing Jim do an impersonation of him, Eastwood cast him in two of his movies.

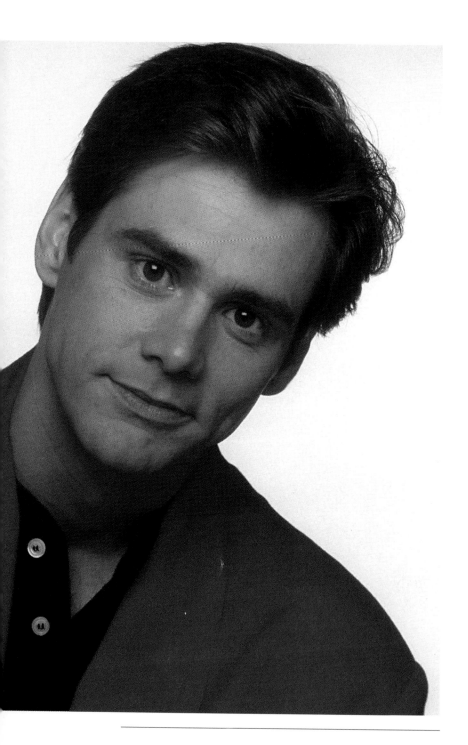

In 1989, Jim landed a part as an alien in the movie *Earth Girls Are Easy*. His rubbery face and physical humor were perfect for the part. His co-star was Damon Wayans, brother of Keenen Ivory Wayans. Damon thought Jim would be perfect in a new television show Keenen was casting.

In Living Color debuted in April 1990 to good reviews. Jim enjoyed doing it as well. The show's format let him develop and play his own outrageous characters. He became best known for his character Fire Marshal Bill. Bill would lecture on fire safety. Then he almost always ended up setting himself on fire. It wasn't long before people began to recognize Jim when he went out in public.

He took advantage of his success to tape a ShowTime comedy special in 1991. He followed that with a made-for-television movie. The movie, *Doing Time on Maple Drive*, cast Jim in a dramatic role. He played a teenage boy with an alcohol problem. He and the film received excellent reviews. Sadly, Kathleen Carrey died shortly before the film was made. She never saw the full extent of her son's success.

ACE
IN THE
HOLE

JIM IMPRESSED VIRTUALLY EVERY
director who worked with him. They realized he
had talent. They also realized that to truly show
off all that talent, someone would have to make a
movie especially for him. That movie was *Ace
Ventura: Pet Detective*.

The idea for *Ace Ventura* had
been floating around Hollywood for
quite some time. Several actors had
turned down the role, including
Whoopi Goldberg and Rick
Moranis. Even Jim turned it down
initially. He felt the script was
weak. He changed his mind when
the movie studio agreed to let him
control the script.

Jim Carrey clowns around on stage while accepting the award for best actor in a musical or comedy motion picture for his role in Man on the Moon *at the 57th Golden Globe Awards, on January 23, 2000.*

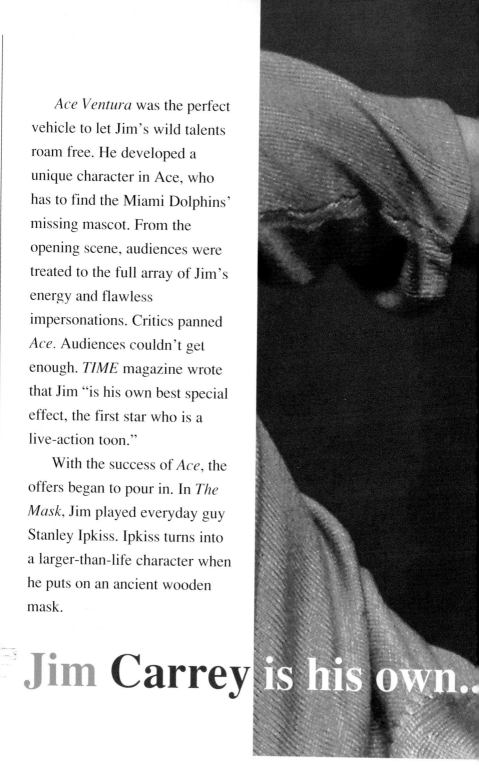

Ace Ventura was the perfect vehicle to let Jim's wild talents roam free. He developed a unique character in Ace, who has to find the Miami Dolphins' missing mascot. From the opening scene, audiences were treated to the full array of Jim's energy and flawless impersonations. Critics panned Ace. Audiences couldn't get enough. TIME magazine wrote that Jim "is his own best special effect, the first star who is a live-action toon."

With the success of Ace, the offers began to pour in. In The Mask, Jim played everyday guy Stanley Ipkiss. Ipkiss turns into a larger-than-life character when he puts on an ancient wooden mask.

Jim Carrey is his own...

...best special effect.

The Mask

Makeup technicians on the set had a special challenge. When Jim's character put on the mask, his skin turned green. Yet the heavy green makeup needed to let Jim's face be free enough to work its magic.

Jim followed *The Mask* with *Dumb and Dumber,* co-starring Jeff Daniels. Jim got a bad haircut and had a cap removed from one of his teeth to better look the part of Lloyd Christmas. During filming, the director learned to leave the camera running virtually all the time. Sometimes Jim would launch into an impromptu routine after the initial scene was finished.

Jim had received $350,000 to do *Ace Ventura.* He received $7 million for *Dumb and Dumber.* Once again, critics felt the film relied too much on bathroom humor. Once again, fans lined up to see Jim go wild.

Dumb and Dumber

Jim Carrey does a routine before presenting an award at the 68th Annual Academy Awards in Los Angeles, on March 25, 1996.

CO-STAR
CRUSH

JUST AS JIM'S CAREER WAS TAKING OFF, his personal life was crumbling. His dedication to his work had long caused strains in his marriage. Finally in 1994, he and wife Melissa divorced. Jim also was coping with the death of his father shortly after *Ace Ventura* and *The Mask* hit theaters.

His therapy came in the form of more movies. He played bad guy Edward Nygma (the Riddler) in the 1995 film *Batman Forever*. That was followed by the sequel *Ace Venture: When Nature Calls*. The second *Ace* was not as good as the first. Jim quickly felt the sting of that failure. He decided it was time to try something different.

In *The Cable Guy*, Jim played a lonely cable television installer who goes too far in trying to befriend Matthew Broderick. Jim intended the movie to be a dark comedy. He wanted to mix humor with a serious message. Fans were expecting to see the usual Jim antics. Even though the film earned a respectable profit, both critics and fans were disappointed.

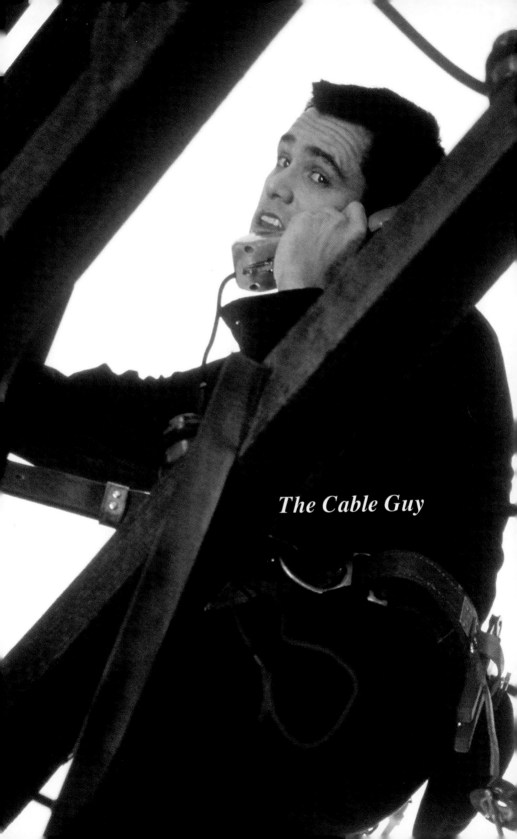

The Cable Guy

The Cable Guy hit theaters in summer 1996. That September, Jim married his *Dumb and Dumber* co-star Lauren Holly. He quickly started work on another film, *Liar, Liar*. In that movie, he played shady lawyer Fletcher Reede. Fletcher's son makes a wish that for one day, that his father cannot tell a lie. The movie taps Jim's many talents to show how Fletcher deals with life when he can no longer lie. *Liar, Liar* earned a record $32 million in just the first weekend.

Sadly, the success of *Liar, Liar* seemed to worsen things in Jim's marriage. In May 1997, he and Holly separated. Jim received some consolation when he picked up two MTV Awards for *The Cable Guy* the next month.

Jim Carrey and Lauren Holly arrive at the premiere of Liar, Liar.

T R U L Y TRUMAN

LIAR, LIAR SHOWED THAT THERE WAS more to Jim Carrey than just comedy. Now Jim wanted an opportunity to show how well he could do in a straight dramatic role. He got the opportunity with *The Truman Show*.

The Truman Show is about a man who realizes that his entire life has been a made-for-TV production. Though Jim shot the film in 1997, it did not appear in theaters until summer 1998. Hollywood insiders speculated the studio held it because it feared another flop like *The Cable Guy*. In another surprise to Hollywood folks, Jim attended the premier of the film with ex-wife Lauren Holly. The film earned respectable reviews, along with a Golden Globe award for best actor in a drama.

There's more to Jim Carrey than just comedy.

Jim Carrey holds his best-actor award for his role in Man on the Moon, *at the 57th annual Golden Globe Awards January 23, 2000.*

While waiting for the release of *The Truman Show*, Jim was approached with many film ideas. One was the story of comedian Andy Kaufman, who died of lung cancer in 1984. In an unusual move, even high-profile actors who wanted the lead had to audition for it. Jim decided the part was worth an audition. He shot his own audition tape in the living room of his home. He wore a peach-colored tuxedo and even used Kaufman's own bongo drums.

Jim's on-target impersonations of many of Kaufman's characters won him the part. Shooting for *Man on the Moon* started in summer 1998. Jim threw himself into the role completely. Others on the set said he was acting like Kaufman even when the cameras weren't rolling. His efforts paid off. He earned another Golden Globe award for his performance.

Jim's next project was another movie, *Me, Myself and Irene*. It's the story of a state trooper who has a split personality. Both of his personalities fall in love with Irene, played by Rene Zellweger. In a repeat performance, Jim began dating Zellweger after the film was finished.

In *Man on the Moon*, Jim completely threw himself into the role of Andy Kaufman.

Audiences got another fix of Jim's talents during the 2000 holiday season with *Dr. Seuss's How the Grinch Stole Christmas*. Filming the lighthearted story was anything but easy. Jim endured five hours of makeup each day. "It was like being buried alive," Jim said of the heavy makeup. After a while it made his skin peel.

He also had to wear huge contact lenses and prosthetics. "One day, about three weeks into it, I really flipped out," he said. "I literally tore my head off. I just had to get out of the costume."

He survived the rest of the filming by taking advice from a former Navy SEAL on how to endure torture. "He showed me simple secrets like rolling a rock in my left hand and pulling and pinching myself in the leg," Jim explained. "After a while, I actually got to enjoy it."

Dr. Seuss's How the Grinch Stole Christmas

*Jim Carrey and
Rene Zellwegger.*

STAYING
HUMBLE

IT'S NO SURPRISE THAT THE MOVIE offers continue to roll in for Jimmy Gene the String Bean. In between movies, Jim, like many stars, struggles with the downside of being famous. He can barely go out in public without being followed by photographers. He's found some solace in riding his motorcycle around Hollywood. People can't see who he is beneath the helmet.

"I don't have a tremendously exciting life," he states. "I just hang with friends, I read, whatever." He frequently visits his brother and sisters in Canada. He also spends time with his daughter, Jane.

Jim Carrey pretends to cry as he talks about not being nominated for an Oscar before presenting the Film Editing Award during the 71st Academy Awards March 21, 1999.

Unlike many stars, Jim has remained humble in the face of success. He attributes that to his middle name. "I figured my parents called me that to keep me humble," he said. "You can never get too cool with a name like Eugene."

It's just the kind of life you would expect from Jim Carrey. He never envisioned any other kind, and he admits he still can't. "I've always imagined that even if something should happen to me, and—heaven forbid—all I could move was my baby finger, a few months later people would be saying, "Hey, you gotta go down to the club to see what Carrey is doing with his finger, man. It's weird!"

Jim Carrey greets fans at the premiere of Dr. Seuss's How the Grinch Stole Christmas, *November 8, 2000, at Universal City, California.*

Jim Carrey at the MTV
Movie Awards *in Santa
Monica, California,
June 7, 1997.*

WHERE ON THE WEB?

You can find out more about Jim Carrey by visiting the following web sites:

Jim Carrey Area
http://www.geocities.com/Hollywood/9090/

Jim Carrey Online
http://www.jimcarreyonline.com/

Carreyland
http://mx7.xoom.com/carrey2/

Jim Carrey Experience
http://www.geocities.com/Hollywood/7993/

Fans also can write to Carrey at:
Jim Carrey
c/o United Talent Agency
9560 Wilshire Boulevard, Suite 500
Beverly Hills, California 90212

GLOSSARY

Impersonation: When a person pretends to be another person.

Improvisation: To do something, such as a comic act, without preparing in advance.

Prosthetic: An artificial body part.

Slapstick: A type of comedy that uses outrageous and unlikely events and actions.

Queen Elizabeth is greeted by Jim Carrey at the English premiere of Dr. Seuss's How the Grinch Stole Christmas, *November 15, 2000.*

INDEX